SCHOLASTIC

Pie Corbett

Storyteller

Traditional tales to read, tell and write

Terms and conditions: CD-Rom

IMPORTANT – PERMITTED USE AND WARNINGS · READ CAREFULLY BEFORE USING

Minimum specification:
- PC or Mac with a 16x CD-Rom drive and 256 Mb RAM
- Windows 98 or higher
- Mac OSX 10.1.5 to 10.6
- Recommended minimum processor speed: 800 MHz
- 16bit sound and graphics card

For all technical support queries, please phone
Scholastic Customer Services on 0845 6039091.

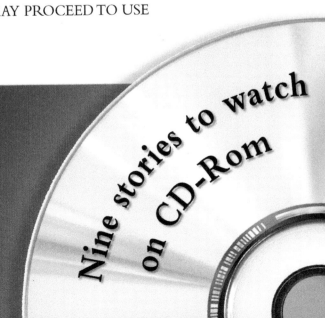

Nine stories to watch on CD-Rom

Credits

'This series is dedicated to all those parents, storytellers and teachers who keep the flame of stories alive in children's minds.'
Pie Corbett

The publishers would like to thank the children and staff at Ebrington, Grasmere and South Grove Primary Schools for their help in creating this product.

Author
Pie Corbett

Editor
Sarah Snashall

Development Editors
Simret Brar / Rachel Mackinnon

Cover Illustration
© Mark Robertson / Arena

Illustrations
© Lisa Berkshire

Series Designer / Designer
Andrea Lewis

CD-Rom Development
Q and D Multimedia Ltd / Adrian Moss/ Atmospheres Ltd

Text © 2008 Pie Corbett
© 2008 Scholastic Ltd

Designed using Adobe InDesign

Published by Scholastic Ltd
Book End
Range Road
Witney
Oxfordshire
OX29 0YD

www.scholastic.co.uk

Printed by Bell and Bain Ltd
14 15 16 17 18 19   6 7

British Library Cataloguing-in-Publication Data
A catalogue record for this book is available from the British Library.

ISBN 978-1407-10068-5

Acknowledgements

The right of the Pie Corbett to be identified as the author of this work has been asserted by him in accordance with the Copyright, Designs and Patents Act 1988.

Contents

For ages 7 to 9

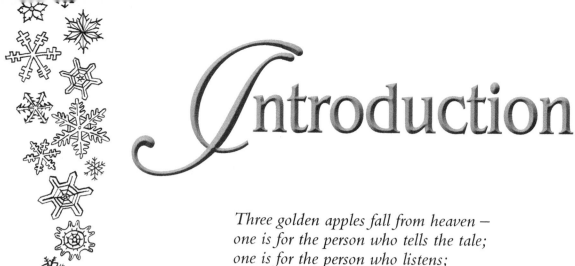

Introduction

*Three golden apples fall from heaven —
one is for the person who tells the tale;
one is for the person who listens;
and one is for the person who passes it on.*

About the series

Storyteller develops the spoken art of storytelling through print, audio, video and the spoken word. The series comprises for 7 to 9 year olds:

- *Dragonory and other stories* – a collection of 17 stories with an audio CD (providing all the stories read aloud).
- *Storyteller Ages 7 to 9* – teacher's notes on each story with a CD-Rom (providing videos of nine stories being told and four storytellers talking about their craft).

The aim of *Storyteller* is to provide a bank of stories that families, teachers and children might retell and develop to make their own.

Why tell stories?

Storytelling weaves a spell that binds us all into one world community. We enter that other world where anything is possible and we can think, feel and grow together. They help us to fashion who we are and to know what is right and what is wrong.

Many schools have discovered that if children learn stories orally, it improves the quality of their writing. This is because oral storytelling develops the children's self-confidence as storytellers, it provides a bank of possibilities to draw upon and encourages the flow of story language and patterns that they can use when writing. If a child knows a story really well, when they sit down to write, it makes the task of writing easier because the brain does not have to compose at the same time as tackling handwriting, spelling and punctuation.

Research has shown that children who are read to and hear stories before coming to school are the most likely to succeed in school. This is because stories help children to sit still, listen and concentrate; they also develop abstract thinking so that children who have had stories told or read to them are the first to form abstract concepts across the curriculum. In addition, stories create a comforting and imaginative world in which ogres can be confronted and our deepest fears played out and controlled. The importance of story has been recognised in the new National Curriculum, which requires children to retell and be familiar with fairy stories, traditional tales, myths and legends from our literary heritage, other cultures and traditions.

As educationalists, we also know that children who are read to or have stories told to them begin to build up and internalise narrative possibilities. Through repetitive, memorable and meaningful storytelling, children build up:

- **The big patterns of stories** – rather like putting templates in the mind. Ted Hughes called these 'blueprints for the imagination'.
- **The building blocks of a story** – openings, dilemmas, action, suspense, resolutions as well as characters, settings and events.
- **The flow of sentences** – because story sentences are different to everyday speech. For instance, *In a distant valley lived a giant.*
- **Words** – not only descriptive language and tricks such as alliteration or imagery, but also story language such as *once upon a time, one day, unfortunately, luckily* and *finally.*

The conditions for internalising these narrative patterns are as follows:
- **Repetition** – the stories have to be heard not once, not twice but at least three times. Children then need time to keep retelling their version in order to gain fluency and confidence.
- **Memorable** – the stories have to be made memorable so that they stay inside the child's mind, a metaphor for their lives. This is why in the teacher's notes I have provided suggestions for artwork, drama, and other forms of exploration.
- **Meaningful** – if the language of the story is to become generative then the children have to understand what the sentences mean. Again, this is why we might paint scenes, act the story out with puppets or hot-seat characters. All of these activities help children to deepen their understanding and appreciation – as well as ensuring that the patterns can be internalised and reused as part of the child's linguistic competence.
- **Hear it** – to internalise a story, it is important that children *hear* them. This may be through the audio CD, watching the videos on the CD-Rom or having the teacher read the story aloud – or most effectively, tell the story. A good telling creates the story in the child's mind.
- **Telling it** – to internalise the story so that it becomes their own, the children have to retell it. Language is learned by 'hearing it' and then 'saying it'. Of course, they will need time to retell a tale until they have gained fluency and confidence.

On the CD-Rom you will find:

Oral performances of nine stories:

1. *The Clever Wish* told by Taffy Thomas
2. *Tattercoats* told by Pie Corbett
3. *Awongaleema* told by Xanthe Gresham
4. *The Snapdragon Plant* told by Taffy Thomas
5. *The Papaya that Spoke* told by Pie Corbett
6. *The Old Man and the Donkey* told by Pie Corbett
7. *Mulenga and the Cherries* told by Pie Corbett
8. *Bimwili and the Zimwi* told by Jane Grell
9. *Lazy Jack* told by Pie Corbett

Storytellers talking about their craft:

Pie Corbett
Xanthe Gresham
Taffy Thomas
Jane Grell

How to tell a story

Telling a story yourself

Storytelling is not as daunting as one might first imagine. We all have a natural propensity towards telling and will have told many anecdotes and recounted many events. Make storytelling easier by following these tips:

- **Choose a story** – find a tale that you like. Start with something fairly brief that has a repetitive pattern.
- **Adapt the story** – this stage is not necessary, but it definitely helps to rewrite the story that you're going to tell because it helps internalise the pattern (and build in any specific language pattern that you want the children to learn).
- **Draw a story map, board or flowchart** – this is crucial. Annotate any rhythmic patterns or special words that you must use (though keep writing to a minimum). Any pictures will help you 'see' the story in your mind.
- **Listen to it** – use the audio CD (supplied with the anthology). Listen and then join in to gain confidence. Listening to the story at least three times in order to be able to attempt a retelling.
- **Try saying the story aloud** – you can have the map in front of you, or just try to see the story in your head. Practise telling the story several times on your own.
- **Now tell it** – find a class and retell the story. You will be surprised how easy it is. Remember that you do not have to know most of the stories word for word.

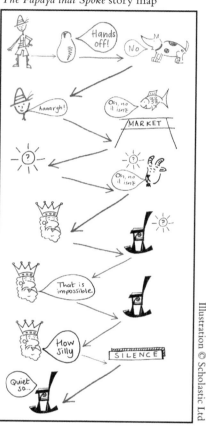

The Papaya that Spoke story map

Illustration © Scholastic Ltd

Helping the children retell

Learning a story takes time. However, the more experienced the children become, the quicker they can learn. Storytelling improves memory. Help the children retell stories by following this process:

- **Listen to the story** – a number of times. Initially, tell the tale and then discuss likes, dislikes, puzzles and, patterns.
- **Draw a story map** – ask the children to listen to the story again and draw a story map or board or a flowchart of key scenes.
- **Watch it** – watch the story on the CD-Rom. Discuss with the children what they liked about 'how' the storytellers tell their tales. Make a list of criteria for good storytelling. For example: speak clearly and loudly; vary the volume, expresssion and pace; use gestures to support the meaning. It might be interesting to compare the written and told versions, which in some cases vary considerably.

- **Activities** – undertake other activities such as drama, writing in role, art, model making, and so on. Set up the audio CD in a listening corner.
- **Join in** – retell the story and encourage the children to increasingly join in. In the end, you may have a unique class version! (With children who have English as a new language or where children struggle with speaking, learning some 'communal' tales word for word can be very helpful. You will find that each anthology has some simple tales with repetitive patterns that would lend themselves to this form of retelling. It is crucial to help the children by using actions for the key events and connectives as well as the map.)
- **Use actions** – use actions with enthusiasm to enhance events.
- **Paired retellings** – put the children in pairs and ask them to retell the tale, either together or by taking turns (they can use their maps or flowcharts). Remember, they do not have to learn the story word for word – they are developing their own fluent retelling. The less confident should stick more closely to the original retelling; be wary of more confident children who may have a tendency to make the tale so elaborate that it loses impact.
- **Let pairs or individuals retell** – and ask the class to evaluate. In this way, children learn from each other.
- **Bit by bit** – with long stories, it can be helpful if children work on different sections of the story, bit by bit.
- **Perform** – when ready, ask the children to perform to other classes in pairs or individually; capture the performances on video or record on audio.
- **Writing** – finally, you may wish the children to move into writing. Use shared writing to show how the story may be crafted further as a precursor to the children's own writing.

Making the stories your own

Once children have a fluent version of the basic story then you can begin to craft the tale. This can be done in various ways, from the simple to the complex. For example:

- Substitutions – change a few details such as names, places, animals and objects. Basically, it is the same story but only a few words altered.
- Addition – retell the story, making a few changes but adding more details, description, events or dialogue. Try not to let it get out of control!
- Alteration – try altering characters or settings or events so that there are consequences. The story stays within the overall frame but may veer in new directions. Try changing the ending or altering the sequence of events.
- Change of view – retell from a different angle (by a different character or as a diary, letter or news report).
- Recycle the plot – retell, but alter everything except for the underlying plot pattern or theme.

Precede writing a new version by drawing a new story map or flowchart. Allow plenty of chances to retell the new story. Model how to do this with a new class version, then let the children draw their own new story and retell. They will need to retell their story at least three times for it to begin to become fluent. Some children will need at least six retellings before writing.

The Clever Wish

About the story

There are many versions of this popular story. They all involve the main character rescuing or helping an animal and being granted one wish, but ending up having all his/her wishes successfully fulfilled.

Getting to know the story well

After sharing the story, use the following activities to embed the story in the children's minds.

Drama

■ Hot-seat the main character – first, before he meets the unicorn and then after his wish.

Art

■ Paint pictures of the unicorn and other such magical creatures who might be prepared to grant a magical wish.

Discuss

■ Did the main character deserve such luck?

Story behind the story

■ Tell or read to the children the well-known story of *The Three Wishes* in which the wishes are wasted.

Retelling the story aloud

■ This is a simple version that would be fairly easy to retell aloud in the children's own words. They need to make sure that they have learned the wish in which all three things are gained in one in order to process with fluency.

■ Display a version of the flowchart to help the children structure their telling.

■ Suggest to the children that they learn to pause and ask their audience how the man should use his one wish.

From telling to writing

■ When the children can tell their story fluently, ask them to write it down. They might want to write a new version of the story. They could try writing the story in the present tense rather than recounting what happened.

Watch it
Watch the video of Taffy Thomas telling *The Clever Wish* on the CD-Rom.

> An unlucky man is poor, childless and has a blind mother.

> He sees a trapped unicorn and is about to shoot it when it offers him a wish to set it free.

> He knows he wants money, a baby and eyesight for his mother.

> He wishes for all three in one.

> His wish comes true.

Jack Foretells the Future

About the story

There are many stories about Jack, who is often portrayed as being the cleverest of three brothers. Sometimes he seems daft but he always wins in the end. His partner in many stories is called Mary.

Getting to know the story well

After sharing the story, try out the following activities.

Drama

- In pairs, create a freeze frame at any point in the story, with one child in role as Jack and another as the farmer. Interview both characters to see what they are thinking.

Writing in role

- Make a list of other silly things that the farmer might do.

Art

- Create a cartoon of the story, like a comic for younger children.

Discuss

- Read carefully and list clues that tell us about the two characters.

Story behind the story

- Find other Jack stories to retell.

Retelling the story aloud

- When the children are familiar with the story, display the flowchart and encourage them to tell the story in pairs.
- Work with the children on their comic timing at the end of the story.

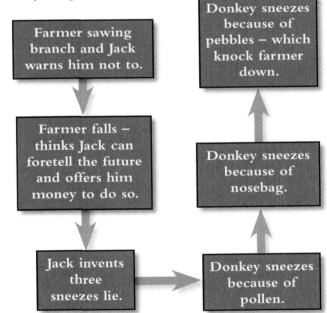

From telling to writing

- Once the children are fluently retelling the story, encourage them to write their version down. Challenge some children to recast the tale in a different setting and time. They will need to think of something daft that the 'silly' character does at the beginning. Then they will have to think of what the 'Jack' figure foretells.

Dragonory

About the story

Jess Smith is part of the travelling tradition. She writes that *Dragonory* is a camp fire story that traveller children 'cut their teeth on'. This is really a simple journey story about 'the way that is blocked' – in this case not by a troll, as in *The Three Billy Goats Gruff*, but by a dragon. To get past the dragon a riddling contest is held. In a nice touch at the end, the main character rescues Dragonory.

Getting to know the story well

Read aloud, or tell, the story to the class. Use the following activities to help the children get to know the story well prior to learning to tell it.

Drama

- Re-enact sitting round a camp fire in the classroom or hall – or if it is sunny enough, outside. Experiment with the children beginning to tell stories round the 'fire'.
- Role-play the riddle scene. Encourage the children to use their own riddles.

Writing in role

- Write, or collect, riddles to outwit a dragon. Create a class riddle book.
- Write a poster warning travellers to pay up if they wish to cross the bridge.

Art

- Paint and make models of dragons.
- Design and make a rickety bridge out of sticks.

Research

- Visit Jess Smith's website at **www.jesssmith.co.uk** to see images of her travelling childhood on her homepage.

Discuss

- Discuss how there is a preamble to the story. Look at how the language changes as the storyteller takes over. Then look for another change where Dragonory starts to speak.
- As a class, create the story of how Dragonory came to build the bridge.

Retelling the story aloud

- The riddles are a good starting point for telling here. As a warm-up before telling the whole story, the children can begin by telling riddles to each other. They can choose their favourite riddles to use in their version of the story.
- When they're ready to start telling the story, work through the story together, spending some time honing it to its bare bones. You could skip the preambles and just retell the key story.
- Create a flowchart for the story (it will look something like the following) and encourage the children to use it – or their own version of it – to retell *Dragonory* in pairs.

- Share Jess Smith's story-telling advice with the children:
  'No matter how outrageous the characters are, believe in them. Don't talk from the throat but from the abdomen. If there's screaming: scream. If there's crying: big sobs. Laugh from the soles of your feet.'

From telling to writing

- Provide sufficient time for the children to refine their story. Once they can tell it fluently, they will be ready to start writing it down. Some children might want to develop their story further when they write it down.
- It might help to build a description of the dragon, perhaps through Toki's eyes:

  Toki stared at the dragon. It was taller than him and glared with scarlet eyes that seemed to dig deep into his very soul. Its scales shone with blues and greens and as it moved they creaked like metallic armour. Its tail swished side to side like a vast, spiny snake. When the dragon opened its mouth to speak, Toki saw the jagged teeth like a thousand daggers or the teeth of a giant's saw...

- The story could be retold from the perspective of the dragon in the first person or the third person: *Dragonory stood at the edge of the river and stared at the boy.*

Tattercoats

About the story

This story is based upon a version found in Joseph Jacob's famous collection *English Fairy Tales* from over 100 years ago. It is a variation of the Cinderella story. In this version, Pie Corbett has tried to make more of the grandfather's sadness that stops him from being loving and at the end offers hope that the granddaughter's love will lead to forgiveness and reconciliation.

Getting to know the story well

Watch, read or tell the story of *Tattercoats* to the children. Use these activities to improve their knowledge and understanding of the story.

Watch it
Watch the video of Pie Corbett telling *Tattercoats* on the CD-Rom.

Drama

- Role-play what the fine ladies said about Tattercoats coming to the hall and the Prince choosing her for his bride.

Writing in role

- Write a news item about the forthcoming ball.

Art

- Draw and paint the geese, Tattercoats' old dress and the magical gown. Collage would be a great medium for this activity.

Dance and music

- Create a simple dance for Tattercoats with the geese following her. Use a flute or recorder to invent a simple tune to play in role as the gooseherd.

Research

- Compare the audio/written version of the story with the version that Pie Corbett tells on the CD-Rom. Listen to how the told version is not 'word for word'.

Discuss

- Talk about why the grandfather locks himself away. Why can he not speak to Tattercoats at the end? Why might the grandfather have gone to the ball?
- Why is the King pleased with the Prince – what are the good reasons for his choice in marriage?
- Compare the story of *Tattercoats* with a traditional version of *Cinderella*.

Retelling the story aloud

- Tattercoats is quite a demanding tale to tell. Spend plenty of time on a class flowchart for the story. You will end up with something like the following:

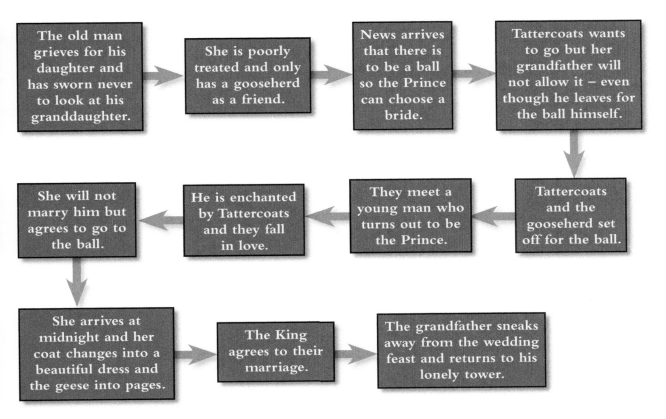

- Get the children to work in pairs to rehearse different sections of the story. Remind them that a told version does not need to be 'word for word' and that they should use their own ideas.
- The children will need to practise over a few days to begin to sort out a fluent version.

From telling to writing

- Once the children are able to tell the story fluently, encourage them to work on a written version. Get them to write over several days, working on each section to increase the detail and atmosphere:

> *Long ago there was an old man who spent his days at the very top of a tall tower. He sat in a great chair, staring out to the sea and wept. He wept so much that his tears carved a groove in the stone windowsill. And why was he so sad? Well, he had vowed that he would never set eyes upon his granddaughter because the day that she had been born was the day that his daughter had died…*

Awongaleema

About the story

Awongaleema is a combination of an Arabian Nights story and an African folk tale. It is better to act it out with the children and use whatever animals they suggest to go on the journey.

Getting to know the story well

Read *Awongaleema* with the children before they carry out the following activities.

Art
- Use different types of fruit for printing, close observational drawing and painting.

Dance
- Create a dance for the scene where the animals become frozen and then use music to bring each creature back to life from the magical droplets of water.

Art
- Carry out surveys within the school to find out the most popular fruits.

Writing in role
- Ask the children what can be learned from this story and what the moral is.

Story behind the story
- Tell the story of some of the other creatures who visited the mountain man. Why were they visiting and what happened?

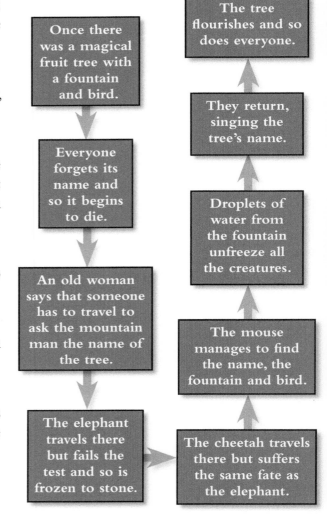

Once there was a magical fruit tree with a fountain and bird.

Everyone forgets its name and so it begins to die.

An old woman says that someone has to travel to ask the mountain man the name of the tree.

The elephant travels there but fails the test and so is frozen to stone.

The cheetah travels there but suffers the same fate as the elephant.

The mouse manages to find the name, the fountain and bird.

Droplets of water from the fountain unfreeze all the creatures.

They return, singing the tree's name.

The tree flourishes and so does everyone.

From telling to writing

- The children could re-invent the story using the underlying ideas. They could invent a magical tree, bush, bird, plant or fountain that provides good things for all the people and animals. However, they forget its name or the song, and so the magic fades and they begin to suffer. To rescue the magic, someone has to travel and carry out a task, such as crossing the ocean to pluck a fruit from a garden. The most unlikely character succeeds. The magic returns and all is well.

The Snapdragon Plant

Getting to know the story well
Share *The Snapdragon Plant* with the children before carrying out the following activities.

Drama
- Take on the role as the Mayor; let the children be 'the people'. Role-play the scenes between the Mayor and the people and the Mayor and the dragon.

Writing in role
- Write up the agreement between the Mayor and the dragon.
- Get the children to write in role as a school friend of the boy. Can they make a list of things that the friend enjoys about winter, spring, summer and autumn? Tell them to list signs for each season to help the dragon know when the seasons change.

Art
- Divide a painting into quarters and paint seasonal images of the dragon.

Discuss
- Ask: Is the Dragon of Winter a real dragon?

Retelling the story aloud
- As *The Snapdragon Plant* is quite a long story, organise the children to retell the story in groups. Display the flowchart to help them remember the elements of the story.

Watch it
Watch the video of Taffy Thomas telling *The Snapdragon Plant* on the CD-Rom.

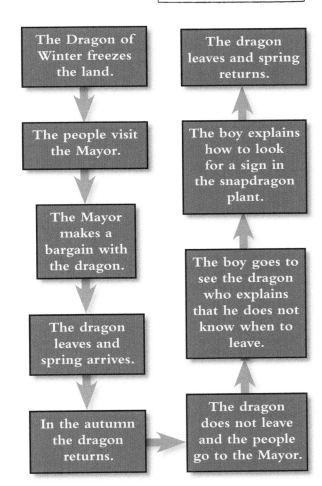

From telling to writing

- Let the children build up their initial description of the frozen landscape. Give them the option of using a different sign at the end.

The Papaya that Spoke

About the story

The Papaya that Spoke is well known in different parts of Africa, though usually it is a yam that speaks. Sometimes a cow speaks or a tree, a fish trap or a weaver's cloth. However, in essence, the story is about someone who keeps hearing things speak. In that sense it is a sort of ghost story!

Getting to know the story well

Start off by showing the children some pictures of papayas (from books or the internet). Once everyone has had a chance to look at the fruit, watch or tell the story to the class.

Drama

- Interview all the characters involved - including the animals, as they can speak!
- Work in groups to prepare a simple re-enactment of the story, using a narrator. Perform the story for a younger class.

Writing in role

- Write a diary entry for any of the characters.

Art

- Present the story as a beautifully illustrated map. Decorate with designs taken from the tale (such as yams, foot or paw prints).

Dance

- Prepare a mime of the story so that it is told using gesture and movement with no words.

Music

- Use a simple drumbeat to add to the 'run' (the repeated pattern, 'he ran and he ran and he ran') and dramatic moments.

Research

- As this is a tale told in Africa it would fit in well to any topic work on that part of the world.

Story beyond the story

- Tell the story of either the farmer or the fisherman – what happened next to them? What happened to the King?

Watch it
Watch the video of Pie Corbett telling *The Papaya that Spoke* on the CD-Rom.

Retelling the story aloud

- This story is simple enough to be learned word for word as a communal retelling. Once the class know the story, move into story circles where it can be passed round the circle and then into pairs.
- Let the children prepare a good retelling in pairs and then teach other pairs in a different class so that you end up with groups of four who know the story and can retell in other classes – thereby aiming to spread the story across the school!
- Display the following flowchart to help the children learn the story.

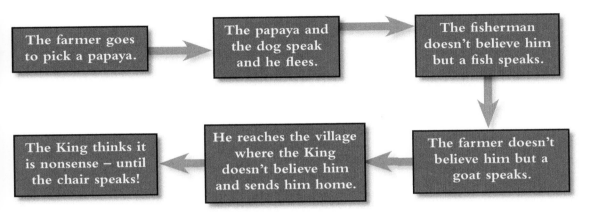

The farmer goes to pick a papaya. → The papaya and the dog speak and he flees. → The fisherman doesn't believe him but a fish speaks.

The farmer doesn't believe him but a goat speaks.

The King thinks it is nonsense – until the chair speaks! ← He reaches the village where the King doesn't believe him and sends him home. ←

From telling to writing

- Once the children can tell the story fluently, encourage them to start writing down their own version of the story.
- This would make a good story for the children to embellish and add in more description and characterisation. But it could also form the basis of developing an interesting ghost story by using the underlying theme of 'objects come alive and speak'.
- To help the children invent a ghost story, tell them to start with a character who is doing something in an everyday setting. However, gradually he/she notices that things are coming alive. Perhaps, at first, it is very slight (for example, an eye on a photo winks) and the character is not sure what is happening. However, it increasingly becomes more stated till in the end a ghostly message appears on a computer screen. The poor character tells someone else (such as a policeman) and is not believed. End the story with the policeman suddenly seeing or hearing something ghostly happening …

> *Mr Jenkins took off his police helmet and began to make himself a cup of tea. He couldn't help thinking about the poor man who reckoned that he had seen and heard things. Ghosts, indeed!*
> *It was at that moment, that the kettle began to glow and its spout turned towards Mr Jenkins, widening into the shape of a metallic mouth. Then it spoke!*

The Liar

About the story

There are many stories that involve lying competitions. In fact, in England there is an annual competition which hinges around who can tell the story with the most lies! In a strange way, all stories are a form of untruth – but the best have a definite ring of truth about them. This story is based on an Armenian folk tale which was originally recorded in Russian, in a village in the province of Ayrarat in about 1884. The author has innovated considerably on the original.

Getting to know the story well

After sharing the story, use the following activities to embed the story in the children's minds.

Drama

- Organise a role-play set in the court. Ask some children to gossip in role as a courtier who saw what happened.
- Ask other children to role-play the conversation between the Prince and Princess before they whisper to their father.

Writing in role

- Make a list of fabulous things that the King might have been bored by. Produce the scroll about the competition.

Research

- Find the original versions of the stories told by the gypsy, tinker, lady, clown and musician. *Bold Mary and the Fox* is a slightly bloodthirsty story common in the gypsy tradition in England and Wales. Listen and retell these in role as the various characters. Helen Frances recommends the Chinese version of *The Ship of Fools*.
- Helen Frances writes that the lady is Scheherezade. Research the stories that Scheherezade told in *Arabian Nights*.

Discuss

- Why was the King bored when he had so much? What did he really want? What words best describe the King? Who is cleverest in the story? What did the Prince and Princess whisper into the King's ear?

Story behind the story

- Retell the story of any of the characters who come to tell their tale.

Retelling the story aloud

- In Helen Frances's version of *The Liar* the basic tale is very much elaborated. An oral retelling might be easier if you trim the tale back to the bare essentials, otherwise the children might get lost amongst all the detail which is not necessary to the narrative. For example:

> *Once upon a time there was a King who was bored. He was so bored that he decided to hold a competition to see who was the cleverest at telling fibs. The winner would be given the prize of an apple made from pure gold. One by one the storytellers of the land came by and told their stories but the King just agreed with their stories and claimed that well, that might have happened.*
>
> *One day a farmer came by. He was holding a large bag. "What do you have to say?" asked the King.*
>
> *"I'm here to pick up the bag of gold that you borrowed from me," replied the farmer.*
>
> *"You liar! I never lent you a thing," replied the King.*
>
> *"If I am a liar, then you owe me the golden apple," replied the farmer, "and if I am telling the truth, why then you owe me that bag of gold.*

- Once the children are familiar with this short version, they can elaborate as they develop their own versions to tell.
- Display the following flowchart to help the children keep track of the story.

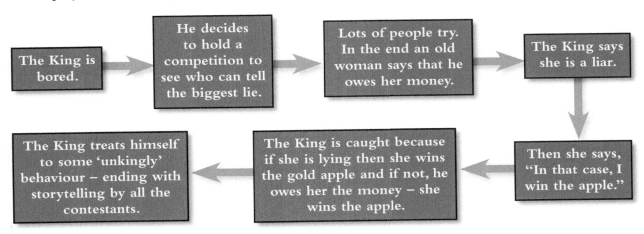

- This story is a useful device for telling some small stories within the basic story pattern. Remind the children to end their story with the trick of accusing the King of owing money. Useful short stories to tell can be found in any collection of *Aesop's Fables*. Provide copies of short stories and let the children choose one they like. Give them time to make a map and retell in pairs until they are ready. Now hold a story competition to see who can tell the best 'lie' or story. Have a golden apple as a reward. Role-play as if telling at the King's court (perhaps with yourself in role as the King).

From telling to writing

- Once the class has had fun with the storytelling competition, this would be a good starting point for writing a class book of short tales wrapped around with the story of *The Liar*.

The Old Man and the Donkey and Mulenga and the Cherries

Getting to know the stories well

Use the following activities to help the children get to know the stories well, prior to learning to tell them.

Watch it
Watch the video of Pie Corbett telling *The Old Man and the Donkey* and *Mulenga and the Cherries* on the CD-Rom.

Drama

- Role-play a scene at the market when the various 'onlookers' all meet together and talk about their encounter with the old man and the donkey, referring to the varying advice they have given. Role-play the scene when the old man and the little boy return home, empty handed not having been to the market. Hot-seat the characters from either story.

- Add Mulenga and his mother to the role-play. After listening to the talk of the donkey, the characters could visit the fruit stall.

Art

- Ask the children to produce cartoon versions of both the tales.

Research

- Use an atlas to locate Zambia. Search the internet for images of Zambian countryside and markets.

Discuss

- Ask the children what they think should have been done with the donkey in *The Old Man and the Donkey*. What do the children think the old man should have said to the onlookers?

- In *Mulenga and the Cherries*, do the children think Mulenga was being clever or greedy?

Retelling the stories aloud

- The repetitive pattern of *The Old Man and the Donkey* makes it a great story to learn word for word and a good starting point for an inexperienced class. Display a version of the flowchart to help with the storytelling.

- Encourage the children to go to town with the characterisation – a very young boy and a very old man. Because this story is fairly easy to tell, it makes a good one to use with an inexperienced class as it will be easy enough for them to learn.
- Enjoy the drama of 'runs' in this and any other stories (the repetitive patterns such as 'he ran and he ran and he ran'). The children can encourage any audience to join in the telling here.
- Ask the children to create their own flowchart for *Mulenga and the Cherries* and to use their charts to tell the story to each other in their own words.
- As they become confident, get the children to add extra detail to their retelling, such as showing how hot and thirsty Mulenga felt on his trip to the market.

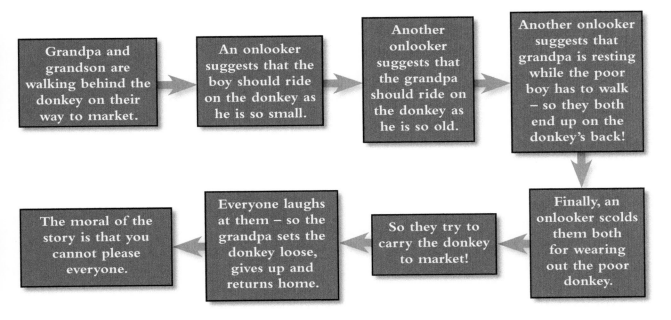

```
Grandpa and        →   An onlooker        →   Another            →   Another onlooker
grandson are           suggests that the      onlooker               suggests that
walking behind the     boy should ride        suggests that          grandpa is resting
donkey on their        on the donkey as       the grandpa            while the poor
way to market.         he is so small.        should ride on         boy has to walk
                                              the donkey as          – so they both
                                              he is so old.          end up on the
                                                                     donkey's back!
                                                                            ↓
The moral of the   ←   Everyone laughs    ←   So they try to     ←   Finally, an
story is that you      at them – so the       carry the donkey       onlooker scolds
cannot please          grandpa sets the       to market!             them both
everyone.              donkey loose,                                 for wearing
                       gives up and                                  out the poor
                       returns home.                                 donkey.
```

From telling to writing

- Provide time for the children to refine their stories. Once they can tell either of the stories fluently, they will be ready to start writing them down. Some children will want to develop their story further when they write it down.
- To strengthen *The Old Man and the Donkey*, the children can build up the characterisation so that it is obvious that grandpa is old and finds the walking hard – and so too does the boy! The children could also use description of the setting to show how hot and long the journey is for them. They might like to choose a name for the boy:

> *The path wound on and up the mountain and grandpa kept pausing for a rest. Simla noticed that his breathing was heavy. The sun beat down upon them and their footsteps scuffed up the dust. "Let's rest under that tree," muttered grandpa, struggling towards a small tree at the side of the road. But the donkey did not want to pause and walked steadily forwards so they had to continue walking. At that moment a stranger came round the bend in the road...*

Spider's Wife

Getting to know the story well
Read aloud or tell the story to the class. Use the following activities to help embed the key elements of the story.

Drama
- Hot-seat Spider, his wife and the other characters to investigate the different views about Spider's behaviour.
- Working in pairs, ask one child to role-play Spider's wife and the other to role-play a friend. Spider's wife should recount what happened, revealing what she really thinks about her husband.

Writing in role
- Write a diary entry either in role as Spider or his wife.

Art
- Find illustrations or images of patterned or brightly coloured spiders. Use these to draw or paint spiders.
- Help the children to create spider webs out of thread.

Research
- Find other stories about spiders. Investigate how such stories travelled between Africa and the Caribbean.
- Make sure that the children understand that milk can be churned into cream or butter.

Dance
- Create a simple dance for the spider and his wife.

Discuss
- The story begins by stating 'what a fine fellow' Spider is. Discuss this statement, considering the various characters' points of view.

- What things did Spider's wife see that others/he didn't see?
- What is the moral of the story? What did Spider learn?
- Discuss the expression 'there's no good struggling against the stream'.
- Discuss the views expressed in the story about the roles of husband and wife:
  "Men are men. They do as they like."
  "That's how life is – there's no good fighting against it."

Story behind the story
- Retell the story from the point of view of an onlooker.

Retelling the story aloud
- Display the following flowchart to help the children keep track of the story.
- Invite the children to attempt a retelling of the story themselves, fleshing out more detail if necessary.

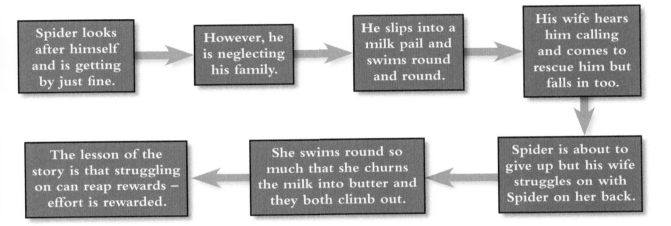

Spider looks after himself and is getting by just fine. → However, he is neglecting his family. → He slips into a milk pail and swims round and round. → His wife hears him calling and comes to rescue him but falls in too. → Spider is about to give up but his wife struggles on with Spider on her back. → She swims round so much that she churns the milk into butter and they both climb out. → The lesson of the story is that struggling on can reap rewards – effort is rewarded.

From telling to writing

- Encourage the children to invent a different story, perhaps using the same moral (effort is rewarded). They will need to think of some way in which Spider (or a different character) gets trapped but escapes with the help of his wife.
- The children should make sure they build their character at the beginning so that he or she appears full of themselves. For example:

> Crow was a fine fellow! He preened his glossy feathers, sharpened his cruel beak and dazzled the other birds with his magnificent voice. He built his nest in the tallest trees and sat up there cawing aloud. All the other birds thought he was a big, strong fellow.
>
> Everyone, that is, except for his wife; but then she saw things differently to everyone else.
>
> Spring came late and the north wind blew snow into the rookery. Crow's wife shivered and the baby crows shivered. Crow was fine because he had enough food for himself. He made sure of that. But his family went hungry!

Little Leo and the Moon Rabbit

About the story

This story comes from Tibet. There are many stories in which the Buddha is represented as a rabbit or hare – possibly reflecting an earlier reincarnation. In one story it is said that the dark shadows on the moon are actually the shape of the hare or Buddha. Explain that a 'sentinel' dog is one that keeps watch.

Getting to know the story well

After sharing the story, use the following activities to embed the story in the children's minds.

Drama

- Try retelling what happened from Painted Dragon and Yak's viewpoint. Role-play Brother Lhakpa telling other monks what has happened.

Art

- Produce a class story frieze showing the various characters.

Research

- Find out where Tibet is located and about monasteries there.
- Find images of Tibet, dragons and sentinel dogs (a breed of dog called Lhasa Apsos).

Discuss

- Talk about what everyone says about Moon Rabbit. How did the dragonfly suggest Leo's idea? How does Moon Rabbit try to trick Leo, and why? What did Moon Rabbit really want? What does the story teach us about friendship?

Retelling the story aloud

- The children should not attempt to memorise this complex story, but should rather extract the pattern and then retell it in their own words. It would be best to work in threes, taking a chunk each – this will lessen the burden on the memory!

From telling to writing

- Once the children are fluently retelling their part of the story, encourage them to start writing. Challenge each group of three to create a chapter for a book.

Bimwili and the Zimwi

About the story
This story is similar to many stories in which the main character is trapped (usually inside a sack). In this story the girl is trapped inside a drum and made to sing – until she recognises her own family and is released.

Getting to know the story well
After sharing the story, use the following activities to embed the story in the children's minds.

Drama
■ Invite the children to role-play the opening scene of the story.

Art
■ Illustrate the story with close observational drawings and paintings of shells.

Music
■ Set the songs to a simple percussive pattern, using drum beats and singing.

Research
■ Find Zanzibar on a map.

Discuss
■ Should the girls have gone back with Bimwili? What message lies behind the story?

Retelling the story aloud
■ This story is in two parts. The children will need plenty of rehearsal, focusing on the two parts in turn, in order to get their oral retelling fluent.

Watch it
Watch the video of Jane Grell telling *Bimwili and the Zimwi* on the CD-Rom.

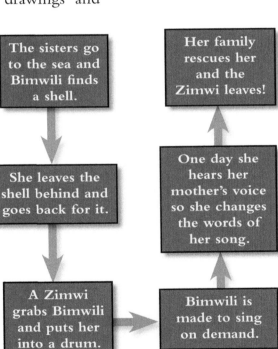

The sisters go to the sea and Bimwili finds a shell.

She leaves the shell behind and goes back for it.

A Zimwi grabs Bimwili and puts her into a drum.

Bimwili is made to sing on demand.

One day she hears her mother's voice so she changes the words of her song.

Her family rescues her and the Zimwi leaves!

From telling to writing

■ Encourage the children to write down their own version of the story. If they wish, they could change some of the details, such as exchanging the drum for a sack.
■ Confident writers could rewrite the story, but set it in a modern circus where someone is made to perform tricks even though they do not want to – ending the story with the main character being reunited with long-lost parents!

Matiwara's Name Game

About the story

This is an African version of the European story of *Rumplestiltskin*. It is found in many parts of the world and, indeed, there are websites dedicated just to this tale! Usha Bahl writes: 'The story was told to me by my grandfather in Nairobi, Kenya. He used to travel to villages to buy fruit and vegetables from the local markets to bring them to the city for sale. On his return we would hear about the villages, locals and markets and any stories he had come across. I remembered the word Shokolokobangoshey. As a child, it seemed like the longest word in the world and the longest name anyone could have.'

Getting to know the story well

When telling the story to the children, you can pause and ask them to add their guesses for the old woman's name to Matiwara's.

Drama

- Hot-seat the characters of Matiwara's parents and interview them before the story and after.
- Role-play the part of visiting the house, meeting the old woman and catching a glimpse of Matiwara.
- Revisit any market role-play carried out for *Mulenga and the Cherries* and *The Old Man and the Donkey*. Recreate the market scene again, this time adding a storyteller telling the story of Matiwara's name game.

Writing in role

- Write a message that Matiwara tries to throw out of the window to a passerby.
- Interview Matiwara and her family and write a 150-word newspaper article about her miraculous re-appearance.

Art

- Paint an image of the small house with Matiwara looking out of the window. Encourage the children to return to the text to add detail of the savannah with its acacia trees and tall sandy grass to their paintings.

Dance and music

- Create the dance that the old woman does around the fire as she chants her name – with Matiwara watching and then creeping away.
- Add simple percussion and use chime bars to create a musical rhythm for the dance. Experiment with different brushes on the drums to create the sound of the wind in the grass.

Research

- Ask the children to research names for girls and boys, especially from a range of different cultures. Are any similar? Which are most popular? Create a class list of favourite names for use in the story.

Discuss
- Compare *Matiwara's Name Game* with the story of *Rumplestiltskin*. (A girl is asked to spin straw into gold by the king and a little man appears who helps her in return for something precious. In the end, she has to promise to give her first baby away. She can only escape this promise by guessing his name.) Ask the children to think about the similarities and differences between the two versions.

Story behind the story
- Tell the story of how the old woman managed to trap Matiwara in her house.

Retelling the story aloud
- Display the flowchart on the board so that the children can visualise the tale as they learn to tell it. Give them plenty of practice in pairs or circles to work out their version. Encourage them to practise saying the name 'Shokolokobangoshey' and any other names they are going to choose to use in their stories.
- Let the children retell the story until they have a fluent version. It can help to tell in pairs or threes – so that each child only has a few sections to develop.

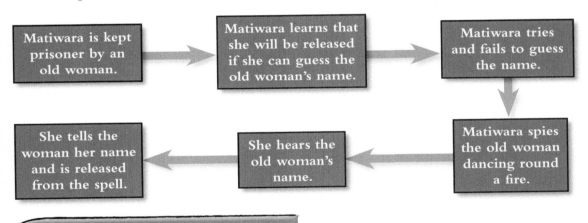

From telling to writing

- Once the children have a fluent version of their story, they can try writing their told version or they might enjoy innovating further. Encourage them to play around with different elements, working out which ones work best by telling and retelling in pairs before writing down.
- Obviously, this version of the story could be innovated upon by simply changing the setting and names. For example:

Day after day Shona stared out of the window. In one direction she could see the dark mountains and in the other direction she could see the edge of the sea with the white waves crashing on the shoreline. Her heart ached to be home but the old woman kept her locked up day and night.

The Monster Over the Hill

About the story

This story is well known in storytelling circles. In many parts of the world there are stories about people overcoming or having to face their fear – and often discovering that it was not as bad as they imagined.

Getting to know the story well

After sharing the story, use the following activities to embed the story in the children's minds.

Drama

- Role-play the opening scene with one child taking the role of the Mayor and all the other children in role as villagers. If need be, you might choose to take on the role of the Mayor to keep the drama moving. The villagers should be asked to hatch a plan themselves which may lead the story in a different direction. For example:

  I am afraid of spiders that crawl on the ceiling.
  I am afraid of dark shadows shifting.
  I am afraid of eyes peering at me in the darkness.
  I am afraid when the lights are turned off at night.
  I am afraid of spelling tests that defeat me.
  I am afraid when my gran's hands are too cold.
  I am afraid when I hear a car screech to a sudden stop...

Art

- Encourage the children to paint or draw a large collage showing the village on one side of the mountain, the mountain in the middle and then Fear on the other side.

Music

- Find an audio clip of some low, slow violin music or something that might be used to accompany the telling of this story – building up to the end.

Discuss

- Revisit the first couple of paragraphs. What does the monster sound like? (Pollution?) Why won't the villagers follow the Mayor's idea of facing the beast together? In what other stories does a weaker or smaller person face danger or take on a task? Ask the children why they think those sort of stories are popular.
- Discuss the end of the story – does fear diminish the nearer you get to it?

Story behind the story

- Tell the story of how Fear came to live over the mountain (or tell the story of other people trying to face Fear but turning back before they see it clearly).
- Display the following flowchart to help the children keep track of the story.

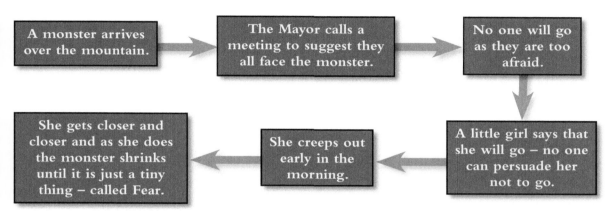

Retelling the story aloud

- This story is an interesting one to tell because the children could experiment with using different voices for the villagers. Also, the end needs careful telling so that perhaps the voice diminishes as Fear shrinks. The last line might be told in a hiss to make it sound more unpleasant.

From telling to writing

- Once the children are fluently retelling the story, encourage them to write down their version. You could challenge some children to write down an adapted version of the story.
- This story would lend itself to rewriting and embellishing as Daniel Morden's retelling is pared back. Each section could be suitably embellished, to build up the end and make more of the journey and its hardships. The children might like to give the girl a name in order to make her more real. They could also try to reveal more of her fears as she struggles up and over the mountain. For example:

    Jocasta grabbed a rock to steady herself. As she paused, there was a rumble from below and she caught sight of a dark shadow moving. A whiff of sulphur drifted up and made her eyes water. She froze for a moment, gripped by her fear.

Lazy Jack

About the story

This story is a well known old tale. In Britain and, indeed, round the world there are many stories of silly characters behaving in a ridiculous manner. The character of 'Jack' often appears in stories in Britain (in other countries he has a different name). He usually manages to win through despite the odds.

Getting to know the story well

After sharing the story, use the following activities to embed the story in the children's minds.

Watch it
Watch the video of Pie Corbett telling *Lazy Jack* on the CD-Rom.

Drama

- Interview Jack's mum about his behaviour.
- Role-play a scene in which the farmers all meet at the market and start talking about Jack and his funny ways.
- Role-play Jack visiting an agony aunt for advice.

Writing in role

- Write a school report for Jack.

Art

- Provide materials for the children to produce the story as a cartoon in a zig-zag book for younger children. Provide the children with the flowchart on the opposite page to help them break down the story.

Discuss

- As a class, make a list of what Jack was paid and what he did with it. Discuss what he should have done. Who is clever in the story?
- Make a list of other stories that feature Jack – in what ways does his character differ? Is he always the same character?

Story behind the story

- Tell the story of the sad girl – this is also a well-known tale in which a girl or princess cannot smile and various people try and fail until the hero arrives.

Retelling the story aloud

- Because this is a very repetitive pattern, the children could learn this story communally, pretty much knowing it word for word. Of course, the patterns may be changed but if you keep listening to the audio version and chant alongside then they will soon pick it up – especially if they all draw story maps. Try gradually turning the sound down on the audio so that they have to take over the telling.

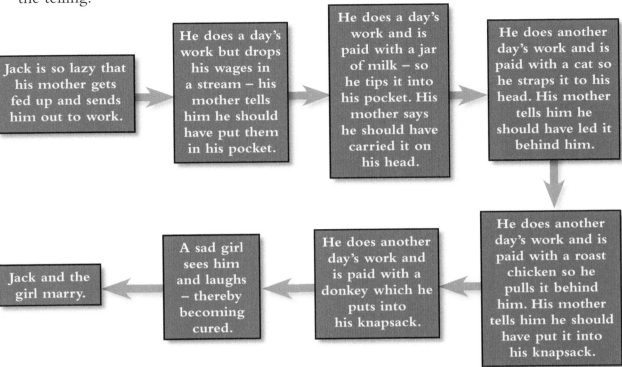

From telling to writing

- Once the children are fluently retelling the story, encourage them to write down their version. This would make a good story to rewrite as a simple chapter book. Each chapter would be a different episode and could be illustrated to make an ideal book for a younger child or to go into the class library.
- Challenge some children to write down an adapted version of the story. For instance, the tale could be modernised and Jack could seek work in a corner shop. For example:

At the end of the day Mr Candy handed Jack a bag of fruit and vegetables as payment for his hard work. It was a large bag and while he was running to the bus stop it burst open, sending all the fruit and vegetables scattering into the road! When he got home his mother was furious. "You should have put them into your rucksack," she told him.

The next day was Tuesday and Jack had managed to find a day's work helping out at the pet shop. All day he worked hard, cleaning the cages and feeding the animals. At the end of the day the owner, Mrs Mac, was so pleased with him that she gave him a puppy that was on its own. Jack remembered what his mother had told him so he put the puppy into the rucksack and set off for home.

At first this was alright but when he was on the bus the puppy began to bark…

Master of all Masters

About the story

This story was recorded by Joseph Jacobs who collected English fairy tales towards the end of the 19th century. This is the only story in 'The Storyteller' that comes straight from an original source, therefore the language is a little old-fashioned. The story is really an extended joke.

Getting to know the story well

After sharing the story, use the following activities to embed it in the children's minds.

Drama

- Begin by hot-seating the character of the girl before she goes to the fair to find work. Then re-enact the scene at the fair.
- Role-play the conversation between the servant girl and her master where he explains what everything is called.
- Finally, enact the scene where the master is sleeping.

Writing in role

- Role-play the maid telling her mother about her new master. Follow this by writing in role the diary of the girl in which she recounts what happened.
- Play a 'swap the words' game. To do this, write a simple recount such as 'How I get to school in the morning'. Take out some of the nouns and swap them over with made-up words. Then read aloud for full effect!

Research

- Who was Joseph Jacobs? What other stories did he collect? Why do the children think collecting stories might be important?

Retelling the story aloud

- To help children remember all the strange words when they retell the story, display the words in large, bold, coloured lettering (perhaps beside drawings of the items they represent).

> Girl seeks job as a maid – and is employed by a 'funny-looking' gentleman.

> Once home, he tells her the words to use for different things.

> That night the girl wakes to find the place in danger of fire.

> She wakes her master and tells him what is happening, using all the strange words that he has taught her.

From telling to writing

- When the children are ready to write down the story, they might choose to keep the central part of the story pretty much as it stands. They could build up the girl at the start, and the end might be drawn out.